Insect World
Walkingsticks
by Mari Schuh

Bullfrog Books

Ideas for Parents and Teachers

Bullfrog Books let children practice reading informational text at the earliest reading levels. Repetition, familiar words, and photo labels support early readers.

Before Reading

- Discuss the cover photo. What does it tell them?

- Look at the picture glossary together. Read and discuss the words.

Read the Book

- "Walk" through the book and look at the photos. Let the child ask questions. Point out the photo labels.

- Read the book to the child, or have him or her read independently.

After Reading

- Prompt the child to think more. Ask: Have you ever seen a walkingstick? Where was it? Did you see it move?

The author dedicates this book to Charles Daniel Ruemping II.

Bullfrog Books are published by Jump!
5357 Penn Avenue South
Minneapolis, MN 55419
www.jumplibrary.com

Library of Congress Cataloging-in-Publication Data

Schuh, Mari C., 1975- author.
  Walkingsticks / by Mari Schuh.
    pages cm. — (Insect world) (Bullfrog books)
  Audience: Ages 5.
  Audience: K to grade 3.
  Includes bibliographical references and index.
  ISBN 978-1-62031-165-3 (hardcover : alk. paper) —
  ISBN 978-1-62496-252-3 (ebook)
1. Stick insects — Juvenile literature. I. Title.
II. Series: Schuh, Mari C., 1975– Insect world.
  QL509.5.S38 2015
  595.7'29—dc23

                                          2014031373

Series Editor: Rebecca Glaser
Series Designer: Ellen Huber
Book Designer: Michelle Sonnek
Photo Researcher: Michelle Sonnek

All photos by Shutterstock except: Alamy, 1; Biosphoto, 6–7; CanStock, 18–19, 23bl; Dreamstime, 5, 8–9, 13, 14–15, 16–17, 23br; Getty, cover; Thinkstock, 10–11.

Printed in the United States of America at Corporate Graphics, in North Mankato, Minnesota.

Table of Contents

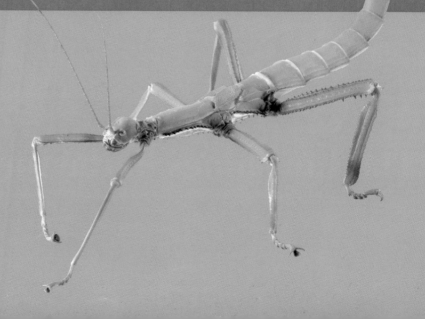

Hidden Bugs

The sun shines in the forest.

A bug hides in the trees.

Do you see a brown bug?

It is a walkingstick.

A walkingstick is long.

It is thin.

It looks like a twig.

A walkingstick is quiet.

It is still.

Look out! A bird!

It is a predator.

The bird grabs the bug.
The walkingstick sheds its leg.

13

Now it is safe.

Its leg will grow back.

Night is here.

The walkingstick looks for food.

It moves slowly.

Long antennas help it smell and feel.

antenna

It finds leaves to eat.

Yum!

Parts of a Walkingstick

leg
A walkingstick's legs point in different directions; this helps them look like twigs.

head
Walkingsticks have small heads.

jaws
Strong jaws let walkingsticks chew lots of leaves.

body
Walkingsticks have long, thin bodies that look like twigs; this helps them hide.

Picture Glossary

antenna
A long feeler that a walkingstick uses to smell and feel.

predator
An animal that eats other animals for food.

forest
A large area with a lot of trees.

shed
To fall off or get rid of; some walkingsticks can shed a leg to escape a predator.

Index

To Learn More

Learning more is as easy as 1, 2, 3.

1) Go to www.factsurfer.com

2) Enter "walkingsticks" into the search box.

3) Click the "Surf" button to see a list of websites.

With factsurfer.com, finding more information is just a click away.